Made in the USA
Las Vegas, NV
14 May 2024

89902663R00069